Flip Flop

A Book Of Haiku By
Miriam Sagan and Michael G. Smith

MIRIAM'S WELL

ACKNOWLEDGMENTS

The authors gratefully acknowledge the following publications in which selections of their haiku originally appeared: *Miriam's Well, Santa Fe Literary Review, The song is...,* and *Whispers.*

Cover painting by Kai Harper Leah

Copyright 2017 © by Miriam Sagan and Michael G. Smith

Book design by Isabel Winson-Sagan

ISBN: 978-1-893003-22-4

All Right Reserved

Miriam's Well
miriamswell.wordpress.com

An Introduction

In a way, all haiku writing is a kind of collaboration. I—a contemporary poet writing in English—am collaborating with an ancient form from another culture and language. My haiku is a hybrid, of necessity. Haiku also speaks to and from the present moment—an instant of awareness that exists, almost paradoxically, in language. Here is another collaboration, between me the observer and the experience, and between the ineffable and the expressed.

Fascinatingly, haiku is not always written alone. Of course there is renga, linked verse, with a group of poets. And there are haiku sequences between two writers. I particularly love *No Other Business Here: a Haiku Correspondence* by John Brandi and Steve Sanfield (La Alameda, 1999). The collection has freshness and intimacy. When I first read it over a dozen years ago I think my brain filed away the possibility of this kind of communication in haiku.

I've always been a haiku writer—and yet I haven't been one until recently. I wrote the traditional grade school 5, 7, 5 syllabic grid as a kid. It was restrictive, but as a budding poet I was delighted to find it. But for most of my writing life, I was drawn more to tanka—longer, more expressive of the self, and perhaps more in a romantic tradition.

When I was sixty years old, I decided to look back and see if I'd written any haiku at all. I had, piecemeal, published here and there, a kind of toe in the ocean of international haiku. I put together a little collection *All My Beautiful Failures* and published a hundred copies to give away as gifts. It was fun, and felt good, but it had an unexpected effect. Suddenly, I was actually focused on writing haiku.

I first met Michael G. Smith because we were both... resting. We were at a weekend Zen retreat with Joan Sutherland-roshi, and I saw someone doing what I was doing, just being quiet during a break. Of course a Zen retreat has silence, but this felt different, and familiar. I was resting because it is hard for me to get through any day. At twenty-one, a near death illness and surgery had left me partially disabled. I was quite used to this, but it made me sensitive to others. I wondered who this person was.

Michael and I became friends and literary compatriots. Our first haiku exchange was, unsurprisingly, about disability. And disability is also about perception—about experiencing things somewhat differently than the usual. We are both also poets of place, and our work became a literal email correspondence when Michael went to Nepal and India. I went no further than Taos, or the corner bistro, but our haiku resonated with each other. The collaboration took a more purposive turn when we both listened to Handel's "Water Music" and responded. Our journeys and writing continued with "A Day in The Life"—the title a homage to the Beatles as well as a directive to observe our worlds.

—*Miriam Sagan*

If I were to construct a frame around my wandering life, I would do so in wood. It would be polygonal. The number of sides I can't guess. But I know I would use heavy woods dripping sap, strips from barkless snags exposing beetle galleries, planks made from woods of old-growth forests—yew, cedar, douglas fir. Dovetails would be made from knotty woods.

I would weave a border around it using twigs from upstart alders rooted on gravel bars downstream from rising mountains. Aware primordial tectonics operate beneath my feet, for I know avalanche and flood too, including a near-fatal dissection of a stealthy vertebral artery, I empathize with the alders. And because of this stroke sixteen years ago, my life changed radically—visual and balance disabilities leave me fatigued and foggy daily. Body-mind consequences acknowledged long ago, I have no doubt my new limitations supported my turn from agnostic scientist to a writer following the Buddhist path where witnessing and reflection are important.

Along the way, haiku bumped me from multiple directions, including from Miriam's Well, the art-writing blog of my dear friend and mentor, Miriam Sagan. Through its immediacy and organic frame, haiku describes a known experience all the while conscious another shoe is waiting to drop. Thus, it is no surprise to me that Miriam and I turned to call-and-response haiku to co-explore our health and disability challenges.

Writing our sequence *Haiku from the Realm of Disability* was fun. Its levity suggested we write sequences framed by airier themes. We conspired to continue while living our lives in Santa Fe and travelling, emailing haiku back and forth across town, mountain ranges, oceans and time zones. Later sequences were composed with music in mind—ancient music, modern music.

After I sent a haiku to Miriam, I waited with curiosity for her response. Every time I was amply rewarded. I'd laugh out loud. I'd recognize and empathize with the sweet poignancy of her verse. I'd craft my echo of hers with a twist, the wandering frame of my life enlarging.

Miriam suggested the title of this volume. Flip-flops are my favorite footwear. I am not surprised she knew. Please enjoy flip-flopping along with our co-journey.

—*Michael G. Smith*

FROM THE REALM OF DISABILITY

sky-blue piñata

my walking stick

adequate

tap of my cane

accompanies me –

autumn crickets

the doctor counts my pulse again sunflowers bloom

early evening some things we won't talk about

cloudless sunrise

sparrows gather

in the birdbath

old friends

could be deep in mountains

if I could go

Manhattan canyons –

mini dress and sneakers

I can run in

one flip-flop, feet in the clouds

maybe I'm still asleep, red monolith

at sixteen

mountains called

and call again

stars silent

a daily nap

peps me up

almost hit two doves

in the road, Our Lady

of Sorrows

I stumble

on slippery river rock–

my niece catches tadpoles

regarding

the stoned teenager–

pink hollyhocks

rosé dawn

over dark mountain –

walking the dog

inhaling turquoise

even as my breath

catches

new waters

remembering

perfect flip turns

scar cuts a new coastline across my thorax

parade passing stuck in traffic

after fiesta

truck washing the street–

a lost red scarf

planting fruit trees

others will

enjoy

the peach tree

she gave me

drops orange leaves

the check engine light

reminds me to call

the doctor

like a child

I hold my breath

passing the graveyard

and yet on the path ahead fireflies

tears blur the line of the prayer

one-hand gassho to the stroked man in rehab

wordless

an empty sky

waits for snow

at Milagro's

speaking French with the girl

the car engine cools

San Luis Valley–

driving at night, across

flat vastness again

star-studded soak

at Valley View Hot Springs

hoping to see you

Vega

glittering west, above

the parking lot

boulder rock stone pebble the smallest grain trips me up

lines in my palm and Rand McNally atlas showed where I'd been passwords and pins

on slips of paper–

gold and orange aspens

wondering

what I'd do differently–

praying mantis

Mountain To Mountain—
Taos and Nepal

before snow

burning the fields–

Taos mountain

Nepal's Head in the Sky

Tibet's Holy Mother–

Everest feels small

dusk

behind white curtains

piñon smoke

dal bhat

cooked over wood coals

today's hunger quenched

in the mirror
a glimpse
of emptiness

shaving,
eyes on
silver bowl

knitting,

my thoughts

unravel the past

the old way–

her parents offer

me money

an ancient story

the river wears the canyon

down

Himalayas

rise

with each earthquake

dream tossed

in rumpled

sheets

the tea house

promised hot showers

bucket bath tonight

dawn

of the shortest days

still streaks pink

mother's necklace

eternally

white

from the air

Gaya's lights

are few

colored globes

at the Tune-Up cafe, snow

changes everything

hospital rising

near the village spring

mother bathes newborn

grown, beautiful

the child I bore beneath

the moon's eclipse

women thresh millet

outside

the restaurant

a giant frosted cake

I do-don't-have

everything I need

walking kora

clockwise

greens and fried rice

what called my name?

just an empty street

full of cold wind

as I type

a man sweeps

last year's leaves

some true affection

between the couple

I glance at

U.S. cafe chai–
masala tea?
naaaahhhh

drum designs
on the pueblo
water tower

stupa practices –

walking meditation

street dog vets

red chiles

from the back of a truck

New Year's Day

riding the river

back first

on an inner tube

we can bicker

about the route

we're already on

little girl's gift
in a tiny clay pot–
forget-me-nots

my father's book
on "Tyranny"–inscribed
in his own hand

hired car

leaving the village

new friends crying

green tea–

forgetting

when to bow

driving along

the river

blurred snapshots

so empty–

pale sky

without cranes

refugee camp –
bead and bone
bracelets

sending a check
for refugees who look
like my grandmother

China's money–

no papers

for Tibetans

instant when the bowl

falls and breaks, an angry word

you can't take back

bamboo scaffold

climbs

the fallen stupa

the neighbor's

Christmas lights are down,

a dreamless sleep

monks chanting

shoeless boy tugs

my sleeve

luckily not

crossing the road –two white hens

black rooster

dusty trail

chasing

yak bells

my mother

hangs up the phone, repeating

"I can't hear you"

a stop to watch

the watermill

grind corn

I hear the house breath,

the bare trees

myself

haiku up

the gompa steps

haiku down

counting syllables

I haven't heard a word

you've said

A Day In the Life

just had breakfast with a vegetarian in the stockyards...

twenty-eight dead

in Kabul

DOW futures up

we make a vow

to not discuss politics

until next time

$x + 1 = x$

some things in life

have no solutions

quarrel over, play

"Ain't No Mountain High Enough"

for you

blueberries sunk

to the muffin's bottom

I flip it over

curve billed thrasher

on the mailbox,

its two-note call arrives

out of the emptiness she steps into my life

friend in chemo
I get stoned
too

trees budded out,
what will I find
at dawn

pow wow dancer
in feathered headdress
checks his cell phone

mirror glance,
the jingle dancer takes
one last stitch

a new scrabble word

hooks onto others

expands the board

walking

the labyrinth–

her nasty jab

how glad I am

I wasn't the one

to say that

despite everything

soup

with carrots

spring gusts

raked leaves

a memory

a stranger's

scoliosis, my old

massage training

black tea afternoon

not my usual

sugar

thinking about

the weaver, barefoot on

Persian rug

nothing distant
about her voice
on the phone

cumulus sky
I peer blankly at
my dim acquaintance

two sides to the page

my scribbles

on one

where is Monet?

Oklahoma haystacks

in the rain

our framed picture

carefully ensconced

in bubble wrap

ROBERT JOHNSON

one golden sidewalk note

on Beale Street

behind thick clouds

swift Mercury

transits the sun

peach orchard blooming

still, century and a half

after Shiloh

raven flies off
squirming fluff of grey
dangling from in its beak

Union dead buried
in the grassy mound –
long time gone

packed for Goodwill

no small things

searching for a mustard seed

my mother's demented

answer to a question

I never asked

a friend's anxiety

attacks

still the buzzing bees

mulch on the sidewalk

towhees at play

again

the overgrown road

that seems to go nowhere

does

breakfast table

dinosaurs

pancakes half-eaten!!!

tiny bird nesting

in a rolled up shade

night train

WATER MUSIC

background kettledrums

rolling riverrock

blood in the veins

ordered garden beds

a baroque score

torn in spring wind

tasting the last
of last years' dried apples
the tree blooms

snowflakes falling
over my lettuce planting hopes,
notes pour allegro

a slow moment observed, lilacs opening without a minute hand

edging off the eave, a raindrop takes its chance

that long-gone cloud

left behind

a red rose

take my ashes

to the Pacific

they won't dance alone

an escapee,
Inky the Octopus
finds the grail to the sea

tea kettle whistling
water's metamorphosis
like a recurring dream

Kew Gadens—
a lily pad big enough to
float a baby on

hot spring pool along
the Gila's bank
howling dog

sutra says "like a lotus from muddy water"-me

foraging along

the sacred Bagmati

gods and pigs

a melody

as Chinese elm seeds

land as weeds

all air

Aquarius–

autumn rain predicted

crossing

our dry river, a cascade

of feeling

Bowling Alley Rapids–

river otter makes

it look easy

a fountain

plays catch

with sunlight

my snowball floats – sutra says "water and ice are the same"

sea level

the cities of the future

at low tide

centuries of lake

ooze between

our boy toes

a fossil shell

now high on

Mt. Meru

About the Authors

Miriam Sagan's haiku books are *Dream That Is Not A Dream*, with Elizabeth Searle Lamb, and *All My Beautiful Failures*. She participated in Axle Arts roadside haiku and renga in the Railyard projects. Sagan curated the installation of three metal signs on Santa Fe's westside which spell out a haiku by Chiyo-Ni. Her haiku have appeared on earrings, chairs, windows, ceramic sculpture, weathergrams, and in numerous publications internationally. She blogs at Miriam's Well (http://miriamswell.wordpress.com).

Michael G. Smith is a chemist. His poetry, tanka, haiku and haibun have been published in many literary journals and anthologies. *The Dark is Different in Reverse* was published by Bitterzoet Press in 2013. *No Small Things* was published by Tres Chicas Books in 2014. *The Dippers Do Their Part*, a collaboration with visual artist Laura Young of haibun and katagami from their Shotpouch Cabin residency sponsored by the Spring Creek Project (Oregon State University), was published by Miriam's Well in 2015.